T0198412

Little Brothers are Annoying

Anaiyah Reneé Alexander

To order additional copies of this book, contact:
Xlibris
844-714-8691
www.Xlibris.com
Orders@Xlibris.com

ISBN: Softcover   978-1-6641-6272-3
         EBook   978-1-6641-6271-6

Interior Image Credit: Sidra Mehmood

Print information available on the last page

Rev. date: 03/16/2021

Naiyah Pie,

To say that you're amazing would be an understatement. You have been ready to take on the world since you began studder stepping at just eight months and demanding to want to know what at *two*! To bring this book to life for you brings me so much joy. Although he drives you crazy at times. the bond between you and your Ty Ty is beyond anything I could have ever hoped for. I am forever thankful, grateful and blessed for the gift of you both! Continue to be great and make me proud. Look out for your brother always. I love you more!

Xoxo,
Mommy

If your mom and dad are like mine, they probably told you that having a little brother was going to be great!

At first, I was excited. I thought I was going to be the best big sister ever!

Who would ever think such a little baby brother would drive you so crazy!

And they smell awful!

But little brothers just do *not* look good in tutus...

And they definitely do not use their manners at tea parties!

Little brothers do not understand that Cinderella is a princess

and not a WWE wrestler...ugh!

When I come home with a treat from school, my mom always makes me share it with my little brother.

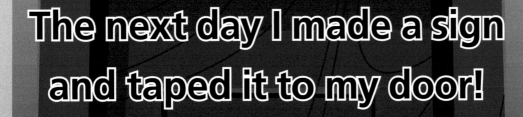

The next day I made a sign
and taped it to my door!

Sometimes, none of my friends are home to play but I can always count on my brother to cheer me up and keep me company.

My brother even lets me pick out my favorite shows for us to watch on tv.

I guess what I should say...is that little brothers are the best!

To My Mommy,

Thank you for helping me make my book a real book for everyone to read. Thank you for being the best mom to me and Ty Ty. I love you with all my heart

To My Little Brother Ty Ty,

Thank you for always playing with me. You are the best little brother in the whole world. I'm so glad I have a little brother like you! I love you so much!

Love,
Nana

ABOUT THE AUTHOR

Anaiyah Renee' Alexander is an amazing entrepreneur, philanthropist, and now author. At just eight years old she has already accomplished so much. She stays busy making and selling her own lipgloss, doing her part to help out her local community, and keeping up her grades in school. She began writing this book as a school project at just six years old and picked it back up to complete it at seven.

Anaiyah is a mix of girly girl, tomboy, and rockstar. Her other hobbies include horseback riding, singing at church, playing the piano and guitar, modeling, painting, drawing, and simply hanging out with family and friends. When she grows up, Anaiyah hopes to become a doctor so she can help sick people feel better.

Printed in the United States
by Baker & Taylor Publisher Services